COOKBOOK

by Melissa Bennett

Table of Contents

Introduction — 6
- Why Sous Vide Is Better Than Traditional Cooking Methods — 6
- Brief History Of Sous Vide — 8
- Essential Equipment for Sous Vide Cooking — 9
- Tips for beginners to avoid the most common mistakes — 10
- Food Safety — 14

Chapter 1 - Sous Vide Cooking Charts — 16

Chapter 2 - Sous Vide Recipes — 22

Sous Vide Vegetables — 22
- Root Vegetable Mash — 22
- Garlic Parmesan Broccolini — 23
- Bacon Brussels Sprouts — 24
- Sous Vide Glazed Carrots — 25
- Mexican Street Corn — 26
- Asparagus with Hollandaise — 27
- Curried Acorn Squash — 28
- Radish Feta Salad — 29
- Honey Glazed Purple Carrots — 30
- Potato Salad — 31

Poultry — 33
- Chicken Cordon Bleu — 33
- Turkey Burgers — 34
- Aromatic Chicken — 35
- Chicken Wings — 37
- Fried Chicken — 38
- Mediterranean Chicken — 39
- Duck a la Orange — 40
- Chicken Thighs & Herbed Rice — 42
- Sticky Duck Wings — 44
- Sage Infused Turkey — 45

Red Meat — 46

- Sicilian Lamb Shanks — 46
- Beef Stroganoff — 48
- Sous Vide Burgers — 50
- Cumin-Spiced Lamb Chops — 52
- Beef Wellington — 53
- Sunday Roast — 55
- Rolled Beef — 56
- Short Ribs Provençale — 58
- Simple Spiced Ribs — 60
- Spiced Beef Brisket — 61

Pork — 63

- BLT — 63
- Pulled Pork — 64
- Barbecue Ribs — 65
- Indian Style Pork — 66
- Breakfast Sausage Patties — 67
- Pork Medallions — 68
- Pork Osso Bucco — 69
- Pork Knuckles — 71
- Carnitas Tacos — 73
- Tokyo-Style Pork Ramen — 74

Fish & Seafood — 76

- Whole Red Snapper — 76
- Coriander Garlic Squids — 77
- Lazy Man's Lobster — 79
- Salmon with Yogurt Dill Sauce — 80
- Crab Zucchini Roulade & Mousse — 81
- Sole Fish & Bacon — 83
- Crusted Tuna Fish — 84
- Teriyaki Salmon — 86
- Swordfish Piccata — 88
- Sous Vide Lobster — 89

Basics, Sauces, and Marinades — 90
- Sweet and Sour Sauce 90
- Hollandaise Sauce 91
- Tomato Sauce 92
- Cranberry Sauce 93
- Béarnaise Sauce 94
- Creme Anglaise 95
- Basil Tomato Sauce 96
- Hot Sauce 97
- Applesauce 98
- Soy Chili Sauce 99

Drinks, Desserts, and Fruits — 100
- Rummy Eggnog 100
- "Barrel-Aged" Negroni 102
- Strawberry Ice Cream 103
- Lime-Ginger Gin Tonic 104
- Mocha Coffee Liqueur 105
- Tom Collins Cocktail 106
- Cherry Manhattan 107
- Watermelon Mint Vodka Infusion 108
- Bloody Mary Cocktail 109
- Orange-Anise Bitters 111
- Peach Infused Bourbon 112

Conclusion — 113

Introduction

Why Sous Vide Is Better Than Traditional Cooking Methods

Have you ever heard the term Sous vide? No, well add it to your vocabulary Sous vide refers to a simple cooking process even though the term itself suggests otherwise. One of the key methods in this process is *sealing*; it requires you to seal up your ingredients in air tight bags which retains juices and aroma that is usually lost during the normal cooking process. Followed by placing the airtight bag in a heater or cook at the required temperature. Once the content is cooked to the specified time and temperature, turn off and remove give it a quick sear and serve as desired.

The Sous Vide cooking method is particularly useful for most meat kind and seafood when traditional cooking methods are applied to these foods they often lose their original appearance, excess amounts of fat and texture.

Imagine the process of frying chicken; the initial temperature will cause the meat's flesh to become tender and succulent. As the temperature increases, the skin will become crisp with hard edges which is an indication of overcooking, but this is only the skin because sometimes the inside is actually undercooked. This often occurs when using metal pans and ovens; traditional cooking techniques allow heat to flow from the burner to the pot then into the food, or the elements in ovens that heat the air which cooks the food.

The sous vide method originated in French – the French term translates to "under vacuum" – the fundamental concept is not predominantly focused on vacuum sealing but precise temperature control also. For example, an automated heater is able to heat food at low temperature level for prolonged hours. This shows that mastering the temperature that is distributed to the food cooking gives the cook multiple advantages. One of these advantages come in the form of time; traditional cooking requires around the clock monitoring because one slip can result in your meal being overcooked.

The advantages of the Sous vide method have led many cooks to try out the technique and improve the quality of their meals.

Here are a few advantages:

1. Simplicity

One of the drawbacks that often deter people from using the sous vide method is the thought that the technique is a difficult one when in practicality the process is a simple one. The beginning of the process takes up the most effort as it requires preparation. Sous vide follows a linear process once this is mastered the extra time and effort that is exerted in traditional cooking is not needed.

2. Tenderness

Tenderness of food is one of the main advantages sous vide has over traditional cooking. Because the food never gets hotter than the water it is in a low temperature is always sustained throughout the process. Tenderness is retained because the meat cells don't burst during cooking and collagen located in the tissue of the meat is broken down without the protein being heated up so that it loses moisture.

3. Moisture Retention

Moisture retention is another advantage of sous vide because it utilizes air tight bags to keep the food, this container creates a moist environment that preserves features such as aromas and moisture that would normally be lost during traditional cooking methods. This enhances your food because it is now cooked with this added juice, which brings out the foods true flavor and texture.

Brief History Of Sous Vide

The plastic pouches and advanced technology gave rise to sous vide cooking as one of the major inventions of the 21st century. Many years back in 1799, Sir Benjamin Thompson, a physicist wrote a theory on the use of heat control over long periods in the cooking meat. Though that was an idea of the 18th century, he never actually invented machines that could have assisted him putting his theory into practice. The theory was therefore forgotten for over 150 years.

In 1974, a chef by the name of Georges Pralus encountered some difficulties while menu planning for his restaurant. Pralus served as a chef at the three-Michelin-starred Troisgros restaurant which was a famous establishment in Roanne in France for Foie Gras. The luxury food had been a well-liked and costly dish. But each time he attempted to cook a slice it reduced by up to half its original weight and lost its natural appearance. Georges knew that there had to be a better way to get this Foie Gras cooked.

He began to experiment the technique through the use of new approaches. He had heard about the use of vacuum in factory food preservation and tried it. He enclosed the foie grass in various sheets of plastic to make it air-free and prepare the Foie Gras in a heated water container. To his surprise the experiment was successful, and this not only saved the restaurant a good amount of money, to lead to a new cooking technique.

Around the same time that Chef Pralus was playing around with his Foie Gras, Bruno Gousaalt was experimenting on prolonging the durability of frozen beef with the use of the sous vide cooking method on a larger scale. The two, each claim to have invented sous vide cooking, but the truth is it would be better to say they acted upon a concept that was already presented years before. They worked separately until 1980 when they began working as a unit to bring the technique under Food Agency in France to be used professionally.

This led to the establishment of companies like Roux Home Rouxl; the pioneer sous vide factory in the United Kingdom which prepared traditional meals to sell to other restaurants. The long-serving head chef of Michelin-starred was Marcello Tully. He explained that it was difficult that the food was being sent to the chefs a bag although the food was of exceptional quality. To him, the technique was never truly a success.

While employed at the company, he watched the evolution of sous vide technique as it moved from being more preservation based to actually a form of cooking meat completely.

Over the years, sous vide cooking has expanded into so much more and is now a common technique used in many restaurants across the globe. There are even multiple sous vide machines available on the market today for household purposes, so it has definitely come a far way.

Essential Equipment for Sous Vide Cooking

Once you try the Sous vide cooking method, you will see that it's a very simple task. It, however, requires some specific sous vide accessories that are geared towards making the sous vide method much simpler while significantly enhancing the outcome of your meals. The accessories that are generally paired with the varying types of sous vide machine are

as follows:

1. Cooking Bins
2. A Vacuum Sealer
3. Flavor injectors
4. A Searing torch

These sous vide machines accessories are essential for bringing food to their optimum result. The main accessory is the vacuum sealer which is vital for every sous vide cooking. The searing torch is used to add color and add a crispness to food which brings out more flavor making meals palatable and appealing. The flavor injectors are used to boost flavors in your meals to complete the technique in creating a superb meal.

Tips for beginners to avoid the most common mistakes

To help you master this sous vide technique, here is a list of **DONTS** which will prevent you from making common mistakes associated with the sous vide method.

Mishandling fat

We all get mouthwatering cravings when we see advertisements and pictures that depict succulent rib eye steak with fat rendered so impeccably that it would just dissolve in your mouth. The common mistake sous vide beginners make is not truly understanding the structure of the meat. They assume the steak fat is going to act the same way as the meat. When in reality it is a misconception because muscle and fat have varying chemical compositions, which gives you different results when they are being cooked.

When a medium-rare steak is being cooked sous vide style, it is being cooked at a specific temperature which falls between 129 and 134 ºF. At this required temperature, the steak fat takes a longer time to be rendered because of this, many complain of "rubber like" fat or fat that is considered unpalatable.

Here are some tips to help you mitigate against this "fat issue" when using the sous vide technique to cook steak, you can sauté or pre- sear the steak before placing it into the cooking bins. This is recommended for more marbleized cuts, like rib eyes. Others recommend cooking the meat for an extended time ensuring that you keep temperatures within the specified ranges. You also have the option of trimming the fat from the meat or choosing meat cuts that are leaner, like fillet mignon or sirloin. methods such as "salt drying," should be avoided because the result is not typically the best. Also, browning produced by Maillard reaction is good to use as when you are doing your final prep on the grill or stove.

Poorly handling sous vide pouches

Seepage is one of the common mistakes that happen when beginners try the sous vide method. If at any time water from cooking bins enter your air tight or vacuum sealed pouches after they are submerged, you would have failed to be properly sealed the containers and will discover that your meal is now trash worthy. For extra precaution try using silicone bags.

Sous vide pouches are delicate as such you should avoid using sharp utensils tongs. They can cause major damage to the food in pouches by distorting, for example, it can delicate fish fillets and puncture the bags. Some foods with hard or pointy exterior like nuts and asparagus can puncture the bags themselves if extra caution is not used when submerging them in the sous vide pouches.

The sous vide method can come in handy when cooking for groups because it allows you to place multiple cuts of meat or fish in the same pouch. The mistake occurs when the cook forgets or neglects to stir the pouch occasionally, stirring prevents the contents from merging and becoming one giant pouch of connected meat, instead of succulent individual portions.

Another common mistake is floating, the content in the pouch must be fully submerged for it to be thoroughly cooked at the required temperature. To ensure pouches are properly secured, they can weigh down by placing a spoon or butter knife in the bag, using a clip to hold them in place or follow manufacturer's instructions on how to prevent floating.

Forgetting eggs are fragile

Eggs Second to steaks is one of the best food you can prepare using sous vide method. But, if you just throw them in to the cooking bins, this will only cause about 20 % of your eggs to come out perfect the other 80 % will be damaged. To keep your eggs intact, place them in a sous vide pouch and allow it to cook at the required temperature, they'll be intact and perfect.

Letting water evaporate

To avoid evaporation try covering cooking bins with a plastic wrap to ensure that the water that would have evaporated reverts to the bath. Also, always ensure that you follow the manufacturer's instructions when attempting to leave your machine unattended. This can not only ruin your meal because evaporation tends to leave pouches floating or partially submerged which will not thoroughly cook food, and in some instances destroy your sous vide machine.

Overcooking foods

Even though the sous vide method is very simple, the mistake comes in the form of overcooked meals. The food continues to cook after it is taken from cooking bin the only way to stop the cooking process is to place it an ice bath. Additionally, during the searing process, the food can quickly become overdone depending on the thickness or thinness of the meat cut. To get a better handle on the methods read up on others experiences and tips and always follow you machines directions to create your perfect meals.

Over – seasoning

Another common mistake made when using the sous vide cooking method is over – seasoning. Beginners tend to season foods just as they would when cooking on a grill or stove top, and in turn, end up with over seasoned food. Think about it, when cooking in a pot or grill some of the seasonings fall off the food and into the pot, and some even blow away in the steam while cooking. When using the sous vide method. However, all that seasoning remains in the sous vide pouch and is absorbed into the food. So, try not to be heavy handed when seasoning for sous vide. It's better to add only aromatics, and fresh spices before cooking then adjusting the seasoning as needed after the sous vide process is done.

Expecting the same end product, you would get from other cooking methods

Many beginners to sous vide cooking end up disappointed in the mouthfeel and texture and mouthfeel of sous vide meat or the way their sous vide vegetables taste as they are comparing it to the other cooking methods. Don't expect the same result! Try to think of sous vide coking as a new adventure with your food; some products will be more tender, while some will be crisp in texture. It's all dependent on so many variables; the only guarantee is that it will feel like a brand-new experience each time.

Keep in mind that all sous vide machines are unique as such be sure to read the directions each time you are about to use a new machine. This will ensure that you are familiar with all the required settings for different products, amount of water needed, calibration settings, how to clean it after use, and so much more. Always **follow the recommended setting of the machine** if it contradicts what is said in a recipe so as to not damage your machine. Remember the machine manufacturers know best!

Cooking foods that don't agree with your machine

Not everything is meant to be cooked using the sous vide method! Many new sous vide cooks get overly excited with the results of their sous vide roasts or steaks, then begin to throw everything they can find in the sous vide machine then get disappointed with the results. Some products are just not meant to be cooked with gentle cooking methods, so don't go throwing breaded chicken nuggets in your sous vide machine expecting crispy goodness as it just won't work. Don't get me wrong, creativity and experimentation are highly encouraged, just try to keep realistic expectations.

Food Safety

Food safety is something that requires both temperature and time. Interestingly, a temperature that is considered inappropriate to keep food safe might, however, be safe if it is maintained long enough. For instance, some sous-vide fish recipes are normally cooked at a temperature not exceeding 131 F (55 Celsius). Nevertheless, persons with compromised immune are discouraged from eating food that hasn't been pasteurized properly. Expectant women should also avoid sous-vide cooked food, since consuming such food can risk their safety as well as that of their unborn kid(s). Therefore, unpasteurized recipes are ultimately the safest choice for pregnant women.

Clostridium botulinum bacteria normally grow in oxygen deprived food. The deadly bacteria can lead to the production of the deadly botulinum toxin. Therefore, sous-vide cooking should be done under properly controlled conditions to lower the risk of botulism poisoning. Overly, the safest food for consumption should be served within four hours after heating. However,
meat should be cooked for longer in order to tenderize it properly, and it should also be consumed within four hours after cooking. More importantly, the
meat should be cooked at least at a temperature of 131 F (55 C). To pasteurize
the meat properly, it should remain in the oven for sufficient time.

Although pasteurization can help kill the botulism bacteria, the likelihood of stubborn botulism spores surviving and getting reactivated after cooling remains a safety concern as with several types of preserved foods. Consequently, Baldwin's treatise recommends certain chilling requirements for 'cook-chill.' This is ultimately crucial for ensuring that the stubborn botulism spores don't get a chance to propagate or grow. Moreover, pasteurized food should be kept in a sealed vacuum pack for up to a fortnight and at about 37 F (3 C).

Some plastic bags may contain plasticizers that are loaded with endocrine disruptors, which are usually released upon heating. The extent of the danger that is posed by plasticizers is still controversial. But due to improved standards of food-grade plastics, plasticizers have become unpopular unlike before. According to Baldwin, plastic pouches that are made specifically for sous-vide cooking should be food-grade to protect the food from getting contaminated
by the plastic constituents. He further notes that these plastic pouches should
also be heat resistant, recommending a softening point of about 90 C (195 F) or
higher. More importantly, they must have low gas permeability for purposes of preventing freeze burn and for providing adequate mechanical strength.

Chapter 1 - Sous Vide Cooking Charts

The time and temperature that you use to cook your food largely depend on the food itself, your desired texture, and on whether the food will be served to anyone with a compromised immune. The amount of time it takes for food to reach your desired temperature solely depends on the initial temperature, shape, and thickness of food item being cooked, as well as the desired temperature of the bath. But when doing sous-vide cooking, it is appropriate to keep the food at a specific temperature for some extra time and for a number of reasons.

Minimum time

Beef brisket, short ribs and other tenderize tough meats can benefit a lot from longer cooking times. It is also possible to make tough cuts tender, at the same time convert their collagen into tender gelatin simply by cooking the meat at temperatures of between 55C (130F) and 60C (140F) for about 6 hours to 3 days. Below 60C (140 F) there can be increased tenderness after 6 hours due to increased activity of the enzymes. Beyond 130F (55 C), the heat can easily breakdown the collagen into gelatin thus lowering inter-fiber adhesion. Basically, the time taken to tenderize reduces drastically as temperature increases. Therefore, it takes approximately 2 days to prepare a chuck roast for at about 55 C (130 F) in a pressure cooker within less than an hour.

Maximum Time

The maximum duration in which you can leave food in the cooking bins varies depending on the type of food. Some foods like fish, chicken and some tender cuts contain enzymes that will leave food with a soggy texture if they are left in cooking bins for extended periods. The exposure breaks down the connective tissue and inter-fiber adhesion quickly. In approximately 4 hours the chicken becomes mushy and even shorter for fish which may become mussy in a matter of minutes.

This is the reason fish and tender cuts are generally brought up to temperature and served. On the other hand, some tender cuts namely poultry should always be pasteurized since they're more likely to make healthy people sick.

Meat kinds like that of beef and tougher cuts can be left in cooking bins for extended periods because they benefit from over exposure. At low temperatures, connective tissue takes a shorter time to break down which could be days compared to fish and chicken. low temperatures.

Here is a detailed breakdown of different foods, and their particular cooking temperature, and average cooking time.

		PORK					
Tenderloin	1.5	4	134	56.5	1.5 hrs.	6-8 hrs.
Chops, Cutlets			134	56.5	2-4 hrs.	6-8 hrs.
			134	56.5	4-6 hrs.	8-10 hrs.
Roast			160-176	71-80	12 hrs.	30 hrs.
Belly (quick)			185	85	5 hrs.	8 hrs.
Belly (slow)			167	75	24 hrs.	48-72 hrs.

VEGETABLES							
	Thickness		Temperature		Time		
	inch	cm	F	C	min	max	
Root	up to 1	up to 2.5	183	84	1-2 hrs.	4 hrs.	
	1.0-2	2.5-5	183	84	2.5 hrs.	4 hrs.	
Tender	up to 1	up to 2.5	183	84	30 min	1.5 hrs.	

LEGUMES						
Beans			183	84	6 hrs.	24 hrs.
Chick Peas			183	84	6 hrs.	9 hrs.
Lentils			183	84	1 hr	3 hrs.

FRUIT						
Firm (Apple, Pear)	up to 1	up to 2.5	183	84	45 min	2 hrs.
Soft	up to 1	up to 2.5	183	84	30 min	1 hr

EGGS						
Soft-cooked in shell (quick)	large	large	167	75	15 min	18 min
Soft-cooked in shell (running yolk)	large	large	143	61.5	45 min	1.5 hrs.
Soft-cooked in shell (honey-like yolk)	large	large	146	63.5	45 min	1.5 hrs.
Soft-cooked in shell (mayonnaise-like yolk)	large	large	148	64	45 min	1.5 hrs.
Soft-cooked in shell camembert-like yolk)	large	large	154.4	68	45 min	1.5 hrs.
Hard-cooked in shell	large	large	160	71	45 min	1.5 hrs.
Pasteurized in shell	large	large	135	57	1.25 hrs.	2 hrs.

POULTRY						
White Meat						
Chicken Breast, bone in	2	5	146	63.5	2.5 hrs.	4-6 hrs.
Chicken Breast, boneless	1	2.5	146	63.5	1 hr	2-4 hrs.
Turkey Breast, bone in	2.75	7	146	63.5	4 hrs.	6-8 hrs.
Turkey Breast, boneless	2	5	146	63.5	2.5 hrs.	4-6 hrs.
Duck Breast	1	2.5	134	56.5	1.5 hrs.	4-6 hrs.
Dark Meat						
Chicken Leg or Thigh, bone in			165-176	74-80	4 hrs.	6-8 hrs.
Chicken Thigh, boneless	1	2.5	165-176	74-80	2 hrs.	4-6 hrs.
Turkey Leg or Thigh			165-176	74-80	8 hrs.	10 hrs.
Duck Leg			165-176	74-80	8 hrs.	18 hrs.

BEEF								
		Thickness		Temperature		Time		
		inch	cm	F	C	min	max	
Tender Cuts (Tenderloin, Ribeye, T-Bone, etc.)		1	2.5	134	56.5	1 hrs.	4 hrs.	
		2	5	134	56.5	3 hrs.	6 hrs.	
Spare Ribs		2	5	134	56.5	24 hrs.	48-72 hrs.	
Flank Steak, Brisket		1	2.5	134	56.5	8 hrs.	24 hrs.	
		2	2.5	134	56.5	12 hrs.	30 hrs.	

SEAFOOD							
Fish (medium rare)	0.5-1	1.25-2.5	126	52	20 min	30 min
	1.0-2	2.5-5	126	52	30 min	40 min
Fish (medium)	0.5-1	1.25-2.5	140	60	20 min	30 min
	1.0-2	2.5-5	140	60	30 min	40 min
Lobster	1	2.5	140	60	45 min	60 min
Scallops	1	2.5	140	60	45 min	60 min
Shrimp	jumbo	jumbo	140	60	30 min	40 min

Chapter 2 - Sous Vide Recipes

Sous Vide Vegetables

Root Vegetable Mash

Ingredients:

- 1 turnip, peeled and chopped
- 2 parsnips, peeled and chopped
- 1 large sweet potato, peeled and chopped
- 2 tbsp. butter
- ½ tsp. sage
- ¼ tsp. salt
- ¼ tsp. pepper

Directions:

Preheat oven to 185°F. Combine vegetables, butter, sage, salt, and pepper in a bag. Seal and place in water bath. Cook 3 hours. Pour contents of bag into a pan. Reduce liquid to a syrup. Pour the vegetables into a bowl and mash thoroughly. Season to taste with additional salt, pepper, and butter if desired.

Serves: 4   **Prep Time:** 30mins   **Cook Time:** 3hrs 30mins

Calories: 145   **Protein:** 1.9g   **Carbs:** 22.3g   **Fat:** 6.1g

Garlic Parmesan Broccolini

Ingredients:

- 1 bunch broccolini, washed and trimmed
- 1 tbsp. butter
- 1 clove garlic, crushed
- ¼ tsp. salt
- ¼ tsp. pepper
- 2 tbsp. grated Parmesan

Directions:

Preheat the water bath to 185°F. Combine broccolini, butter, garlic, salt, and pepper in a bag. Seal and place in water bath. Cook 30 minutes. Remove to plate and sprinkle with Parmesan.

Serves: 4   **Prep Time:** 10mins   **Cook Time:** 30mins

Calories: 62   **Protein:** 4.7g   **Carbs:** 4.8g   **Fat:** 3.6g

Bacon Brussels Sprouts

Ingredients:

- Brussels sprouts (1 lb., trimmed, halved)
- 2 tbsp. butter
- 2 ounces thick-cut bacon, fried and chopped
- 2 cloves garlic, minced
- ¼ tsp. salt
- ¼ tsp. pepper

Directions:

Preheat the water bath to 183°F. Combine all your ingredients in a large Ziploc bag. Seal and place in water bath. Cook 1 hour. Meanwhile, preheat oven to 400°F. After 1 hour has passed, transfer Brussels sprouts onto a lined baking tray. Set to bake until nicely roasted (about 5 minutes). Enjoy!

Serves: 4   **Prep Time: 20mins**   **Cook Time: 1hrs 5mins**

Calories: 230   **Protein: 4g**   **Carbs: 10.8g**   **Fat: 20.2g**

Sous Vide Glazed Carrots

Ingredients:

- 1 lb. carrots, peeled and cut into chunks
- 2 tbsp. unsalted butter
- 1 tbsp. granulated sugar
- Kosher salt
- Freshly ground black pepper
- 1 tbsp. parsley, chopped

Directions:

Set Sous Vide machine to 183 degrees F. Combine all your ingredients into a vacuum seal bad and seal. Set to cook in the sous vide machine until fork tender (about 1 hr.). Empty the ingredients into a skillet over medium heat and allow to reduce into a glaze. Enjoy

Serves: 4   **Prep Time: 12mins**   **Cook Time: 8hrs**

Calories: 100   **Protein: 1.1g**   **Carbs: 11.1g**   **Fat: 6.1g**

Mexican Street Corn

Ingredients:

- 2 ears of corn, shucked
- 2 tbsp. cold butter
- Kosher salt
- Fresh ground pepper
- 1/4 cup mayonnaise
- 1/2 tbsp. Mexican-style chili powder
- 1/2 tsp. finely grated lime zest
- ¼ cup crumbled Cotija cheese
- ¼ cup fresh chopped cilantro
- Lime wedges, for serving

Directions:

Set Sous Vide Cooker to 183 degrees F. Combine your butter and corn in to vacuum seal bag then set to cook in the sous vide cooker, and allow it to cook for 30 minutes. Combine all your remaining ingredients, except cheese, in a small bowl. Add your cheese to another plate. Dip each corn ear in your mayo mixture then roll in cheese. Season to taste and enjoy!

Serves: 2   **Prep Time: 5mins**   **Cook Time: 30mins**

Calories: 388   **Protein: 10.1g**   **Carbs: 33.7g**   **Fat: 26.7g**

Asparagus with Hollandaise

Ingredients:

- 1 bunch asparagus, trimmed
- Sous Vide Hollandaise

Directions:

Preheat the water bath to 145°F. Place bagged sauce in the bath. Set timer for 30 minutes. When the timer has 12 minutes remaining, bag and seal asparagus. Place in water bath and cook for the remaining 10-12 minutes. Remove cooked asparagus from the bath. Arrange on plate. Blend sauce until smooth. Pour over asparagus.

Serves: 4 **Prep Time: 20mins** **Cook Time: 30mins**

Calories: 347 **Protein: 5.5g** **Carbs: 5.4g** **Fat: 34.9g**

Curried Acorn Squash

Ingredients:

- 1 acorn squash, seeded and cut into wedges
- 2 tbsp. butter
- 1 tbsp. curry powder or garam masala
- ¼ tsp. salt

Directions:

Preheat the water bath to 185°F. Combine squash, butter, spice mix, and salt in a bag. Seal and place in water bath. Cook 1 ½ to 2 hours.

Serves: 4   **Prep Time:** 30mins   **Cook Time:** 2hrs

Calories: 99   **Protein:** 1.2g   **Carbs:** 12.1g   **Fat:** 6.1g

Radish Feta Salad

Ingredients:

- 20 small radishes, peeled, trimmed
- 1 tbsp. water
- 1 tbsp. white wine vinegar
- 1 tsp. sugar
- ¼ tsp. salt
- ½ cup feta cheese
- ¼ cup fresh spinach, chopped

Directions:

Preheat the water bath to 200°F. Combine the radishes, water, vinegar, sugar, and salt in a bag. Seal, then place in water bath. Cook radishes 30 minutes, then place in ice water. When radishes are cool, toss with cheese and basil. Serve cold.

Serves: 2 **Prep Time: 20mins** **Cook Time: 30mins**

Calories: 101 **Protein: 5.8g** **Carbs: 2.9g** **Fat: 7g**

Honey Glazed Purple Carrots

Ingredients:

- 1lb. purple carrots, scrubbed
- ¾ cup orange juice
- 2 tbsp. acacia honey
- 2 tsp. orange zest
- 1 sprig mint
- 1 tsp. cumin
- Salt and pepper, to taste

Directions:

Preheat your sous Vide to 185F. Combine all ingredients in a Sous Vide bag. Vacuum seal the bag and submerge carrots in the heated water. Cook the carrots 45 minutes. Remove the bag from the Sous Vide appliance. Open and serve warm.

Serves: 4   **Prep Time:** 10mins   **Cook Time:** 45mins

Calories: 75   **Protein:** 1.4g   **Carbs:** 17.7g   **Fat:** 0.2g

Potato Salad

Ingredients:

- 1 ½ lbs. yellow potatoes
- ½ cup chicken stock
- Salt and pepper to taste
- 4 oz. thick cut bacon, sliced
- ½ cup chopped onion
- ⅓ cup cider vinegar
- 4 scallions, thinly sliced

Directions:

Set Sous Vide cooker to 185F. Cut potatoes into ¾-inch thick cubes. Place potatoes and chicken stock to the zip-lock bag, making sure they are in a single layer; seal using immersion water method. Place potatoes in a water bath and cook for 1 hour 30 minutes.

Meanwhile, in last 15 minutes heat non-stick skillet over medium-high heat. Add bacon and cook until crisp; remove bacon and add chopped onions. Cook until soften for 5-7 minutes. Add vinegar and cook until reduced slightly. Remove potatoes from the water bath and place them in skillet, with the cooking water. Continue cooking for few minutes until liquid thickens. Remove potatoes from the heat and stir in scallions; toss to combine. Serve while still hot.

Serves: 6   **Prep Time: 10mins**   **Cook Time: 1hrs 30mins**

Calories: 108   **Protein: 3.7g**   **Carbs: 19.9g**   **Fat: 1.6g**

Poultry

Chicken Cordon Bleu

Ingredients:

- 2 boneless, skinless chicken breasts, butterflied
- 4 deli slices ham
- 4 deli slices Swiss cheese
- ½ cup flour
- 1 egg
- 1 cup bread crumbs
- 1 cup vegetable oil

Directions:

Preheat the water bath to 140°F. Lay slices of ham on top of butterflied chicken breasts, then lay cheese on top of ham. Trim excess. Roll up chicken breasts with the ham and cheese on the inside. Place prepared chicken breasts inside the bag. Seal tightly and place in water bath. Cook 1 ½ hours. When chicken is done, remove carefully from wrapper and pat dry. Dredge each piece in flour, then dip in egg, followed by the breadcrumbs. Heat oil to 350°F. Fry chicken until golden brown on all sides. Remove to paper towel to drain. Cut breasts in halves, then serve.

Serves: 4   **Prep Time:** 30mins   **Cook Time:** 1hr 30mins

Calories: 567   **Protein:** 46.2g   **Carbs:** 34.2g   **Fat:** 26g

Turkey Burgers

Ingredients:

- 2lb. ground lean turkey
- 1 shallot, chopped
- ½ cup parsley, chopped
- ½ cup sun-dried tomatoes, packed in oil, chopped
- 2 cloves garlic, minced
- 1 teaspoon dry mustard powder
- 1 teaspoon paprika powder
- Salt and pepper, to taste

Directions:

Combine all ingredients in a bowl. Shape the mixture into 6 patties. Arrange the patties on a baking sheet lined with parchment paper. Freeze 4 hours. Preheat Sous Vide cooker to 145 degrees F. Place each patty in a Sous Vide bag and vacuum seal. Place in a water bath 60 minutes.

Remove the bag from the cooker. Open the bag and remove the patties. Heat a grill pan over medium-high heat. Sear the patties for 1 minute per side. Serve with fresh salad and fresh buns.

Serves: 6　　　　　　　　**Prep Time: 20mins**　　　　**Cook Time: 1hr.**

Calories: 212　　**Protein: 30.2g**　　**Carbs: 1.7g**　　**Fat: 9.7g**

Aromatic Chicken

Ingredients:

- 1 cup chicken stock
- 1 tablespoon chili sauce
- 1lb. boneless chicken breasts
- 2 cloves garlic, minced
- 1 good pinch salt
- 1 lemon, thinly sliced
- 4 sprigs basil
- 1 tablespoon olive oil

Directions:

Combine chicken stock and chili sauce in a bowl. Add the chicken breasts and cover with a clean foil. Marinade 45 minutes. In the meantime, heat the Sous Vide cooker to 146F. Pat dry the chicken with paper towels.

Combine the garlic and salt until you have a paste. Spread the past over chicken breasts and top the chicken with lemon. Place the chicken breasts into Sous Vide bag and add-in remaining ingredients. Vacuum seal the bag and submerge chicken in water. Cook the chicken 1 hour 30 minutes.

Heat grill pan to high. Remove the chicken from the cooker and open the bag.

Arrange the lemon slices on a grill pan and top with chicken. Grill the lemon and chicken for 3 minutes per side. Serve.

Serves: 4 **Prep Time: 20mins** **Cook Time: 1hr. 30min**

Calories: 255 **Protein: 33.3g** **Carbs: 2.2g** **Fat: 12.1g**

Chicken Wings

Ingredients:

- 12 chicken wings
- ¼ cup vegetable oil
- 4 sprigs thyme
- 2 teaspoons crushed red pepper flakes
- Salt, to taste

Directions:

Preheat Sous Vide cooker to 167F. In a Sous Vide bag, combine the chicken wing with remaining ingredients. Shake gently to coat the chicken and vacuum seal the bag. Submerge in water and cook 7 hours.

Remove the bag with chicken from cooker. Heat some oil in a large skillet. Place the wings into a skillet and cook until the skin is crispy. Serve.

Serves: 4   **Prep Time: 20mins**   **Cook Time: 7 hrs.**

Calories: 361   **Protein: 14.7g**   **Carbs: 8.6g**   **Fat: 29.8g**

Fried Chicken

Ingredients:

Chicken:

- 3 lb. chicken drums
- 1 tbsp. fine salt

Coating:

- 3 cups all-purpose flour
- 1 tbsp. onion powder
- 1 tsp. garlic powder
- ½ tbsp. dried basil
- 1 tbsp. salt
- 2 cup buttermilk

Directions:

Preheat Sous Vide cooker to 155F. Season chicken with salt. Place the chicken drums in Sous Vide bags. Vacuum seal. Submerge in water and cook 2 hours. Heat 3-inches oil in a pot. Remove the chicken from bags and pat dry. Combine all dry breading ingredients in a large bowl. Place buttermilk in a separate bowl. Dredge chicken drums in flour, buttermilk, and flour again. Fry chicken in batches, until golden and crispy. Serve warm with fresh salad and favorite sauce.

Serves: 8 **Prep Time: 15mins** **Cook Time: 2hrs**

Calories: 357 **Protein: 28.4g** **Carbs: 39.6g** **Fat: 10g**

Mediterranean Chicken

Ingredients:

- 2 chicken breast fillets
- ½ cup sun-dried tomatoes + 2 tbsp. reserved oil
- Salt and black pepper, to taste
- 1 sprig basil
- 1 tablespoon olive oil

Directions:

Preheat the Sous Vide Cooker to 140 degrees F. Season the chicken with salt and pepper. Heat the olive oil in a skillet. Add chicken breasts and cook for 1 minute per side. Transfer immediately in Sous Vide bag, and add remaining ingredients.

Vacuum seal the bag and submerge in water. Cook the chicken 90 minutes.

Remove the bag with chicken from the Cooker. Open the bag and transfer the chicken to a warmed plate. Serve.

Serves: 2 **Prep Time:** 10mins **Cook Time:** 90 mins.

Calories: 318 **Protein:** 13.4g **Carbs:** 1.8g **Fat:** 29.7g

Duck a la Orange

Ingredients:

- 2 5oz. duck breast fillets, skin on
- 1 orange, sliced
- 4 cloves garlic
- 1 shallot, chopped
- 4 sprigs thyme
- 1 teaspoon black peppercorns
- 1 tablespoon sherry vinegar
- ¼ cup red wine
- 2 tablespoons butter
- Salt, to taste

Directions:

Preheat Sous Vide cooker to 135 degrees F. Place the duck breast fillets into a Sous Vide bag. Top the breasts with orange slices, garlic, shallot, thyme, and peppercorns. Vacuum seal the bag and submerge in water. Cook the breasts 2 ½ hours.

Remove the bag from a water bath. Open the bag and remove the breasts. Heat a large skillet over medium-high heat. Sear the duck, skin side down, for 30 seconds. Place the breasts aside and keep warm. In the same skillet, add sherry vinegar and wine. Add the bag content and bring to simmer. Simmer 5 minutes.

Stir in the butter and simmer 1 minute. Serve the duck with prepared sauce.

Serves: 2 30 mins.   **Prep Time: 20mins**   **Cook Time: 2hrs**

Calories: 466   **Protein: 34.5g**   **Carbs: 15.1g**   **Fat: 27.4g**

Chicken Thighs & Herbed Rice

Ingredients:

- 4 chicken thighs
- 2 tablespoons salt
- 4 cups water
- 1 tablespoon paprika powder
- 2 tablespoons vegetable oil
- 2 tablespoons butter

Herbed rice:

- ¾ cup long grain rice
- 2 cups water
- 1 teaspoon salt
- 1 bunch parsley, chopped
- 1 bunch chives, chopped

Peppers:

- 4 red bell peppers, seeded, quartered
- 3 tablespoons olive oil
- 1 sprig thyme
- Salt, to taste

Directions:

Make the chicken; heat Sous Vide cooker to 150 degrees F. In a large bowl, combine salt and water. Add the chicken thighs to a bowl and cover with a clean foil. Refrigerate 4 hours. Remove the chicken, rinse, and pat dry. Combine the butter and paprika and top the chicken. Place the chicken into Sous vide bag and vacuum seal.

Cook in the Sous Vide cooker 4 hours. Make the peppers; combine the peppers with olive oil, thyme, and salt in a Sous Vide Bag. Vacuum seal the peppers and cook in Sous Vide cooker for 30 minutes at 186 degrees F. Make the rice; vacuum the rice with water, salt, and herbs. Cook in the Sous Vide cooker 60 minutes at 203 degrees F.

Heat vegetable oil in a skillet. Add chicken and cook until the skin is crispy. Remove the peppers from the bag and cook in the same skillet with chicken, for 1 minute. Spread the rice on a plate. Top with chicken and bell peppers.

Serves: 10   **Prep Time: 30mins**   **Cook Time: 4hrs.**

Calories: 211   **Protein: 9.1g**   **Carbs: 14.8g**   **Fat: 13.5g**

Sticky Duck Wings

Ingredients:

- 3lb. duck wings
- 1 tbsp. mustard
- ½ cup honey
- 1 tbsp. soy sauce
- ¼ cup ketchup
- 1 tbsp. hot sauce
- 2 tbsp. Cajun spice blend
- ¼ cup butter
- Salt and pepper, to taste

Directions:

Preheat Sous Vide cooker to 150F. Cut the wings into portions and rub with Cajun blend. Season with some salt and pepper. Transfer the wings into cooking bags and add butter. Vacuum seal the wings and submerge in water. Cook the wings 2 hours. Preheat your broiler. Combine remaining ingredients in a bowl. Remove the wings from the cooker and toss with prepared sauce. Arrange the wings on baking sheet and broil 10 minutes, basting with any remaining sauce during that time. Serve warm.

Serves: 6   **Prep Time: 20mins**   **Cook Time: 2hrs**

Calories: 305   **Protein: 15.8g**   **Carbs: 27g**   **Fat: 16.1g**

Sage Infused Turkey

Ingredients:

- 2 turkey legs and thighs, with bone and skin
- 1 lemon, sliced
- 10 sage leaves
- 4 cloves garlic, halved
- Salt, to taste
- 1 teaspoon black peppercorns

Directions:

Preheat Sous Vide bath to 148 degrees F. Season the turkey to taste, then add to a vacuum seal bag with all your remaining ingredients. Seal, and set to cook in the sous vide machine for 12 hours on the turkey related settings. Dry Turkey, and pan sear on medium until lightly browned on all sides then serve.

Serves: 6   **Prep Time: 10mins**   **Cook Time: 12 hrs.**

Calories: 310   **Protein: 57.9g**   **Carbs: 2.6g**   **Fat: 6.4g**

Red Meat

Sicilian Lamb Shanks

Ingredients:

- 1 lb. lamb shanks
- 1 teaspoon salt
- 1 teaspoon pepper
- Juice of 1 lemon
- 1 tablespoon fresh oregano, minced
- 1 clove garlic, minced
- 1 tablespoon tomato paste
- 3 roasted red peppers, mashed
- 1 bay leaf
- 1 sprig fresh rosemary
- 1 tablespoon fresh mint, chopped
- Cooked polenta, for serving

Directions

Preheat the water bath to 140 degrees F. Make a paste of the lemon juice, oregano, garlic, tomato paste, and roasted peppers. Season lamb with salt and pepper then spread paste over lamb. Seal into the bag with bay leaf and rosemary. Place bag in the water bath and cook 48 hours. When the lamb is cooked, place on the bed of cooked polenta and pour sauce on top. Garnish with fresh mint.

Serves: 2   **Prep Time: 20mins**   **Cook Time: 48hrs.**

Calories: 599   **Protein: 101.67g**   **Carbs: 13.8g**   **Fat: 17.46g**

Beef Stroganoff

Ingredients:

- 1.5lb. beef loin
- 2 sprigs thyme
- 6 tablespoons unsalted butter
- 2 cups sliced mushrooms
- 6oz. wide noodles, cooked
- 2 shallots, chopped
- 3 teaspoons all-purpose flour
- 1 cup beef stock
- 2 tablespoons red wine
- 1 cup crème Fraiche
- Salt and pepper, to taste

Directions:

Preheat your Sous Vide cooker to 136 degrees F. Divide the beef among two Sous vide bags. Add 2 tablespoons butter and one sprig thyme per bag. Season with salt and pepper and vacuum seal the bag. Place the bags in a water bath and cook 1 hour 20 minutes.

Just before the meat is ready, heat 2 tablespoons butter in a skillet. Add the shallots and cook 2 minutes. Toss in the mushrooms and cook 5 minutes. Stir in the flour and cook 30 seconds. Add the beef stock and wine. Stir to scrape any stuck bits. Bring to a simmer. Cook until slightly thickened. Stir in crème Fraiche and remove from heat. Add the cooked noodles and toss to combine. Remove the beef from Sous vide bag and slice. Serve with mushrooms and noodles.

Serves: 4   **Prep Time: 15mins**   **Cook Time: 1hr. 20min**

Calories: 367   **Protein: 26.9g**   **Carbs: 13.8g**   **Fat: 22.1g**

Sous Vide Burgers

Ingredients

- 2lb. ground beef
- 1 large egg
- 1 tablespoon dried parsley
- 1 teaspoon black pepper
- Salt, to taste

For Serving:

- Burger Buns
- Salad
- Onion rings
- Tomatoes
- Cheese Slices

Directions:

Heat your Sous vide cooker to 133 degrees F. In a bowl, combine beef, egg, parsley, black pepper, and desired amount of salt. Shape the mixture into patties. Use a kitchen scale to portion meat into 7oz. patties. Place two patties into Sous Vide Bag and vacuum seal. Cook the patties for 15 minutes up to 30 minutes.

Remove the patties from the cooker. Place the patties on a large plate and set aside until cooled to a room temperature. Preheat your grill. Sear the patties 30 seconds per side. Serve with desired additions.

Serves: 4   **Prep Time: 15mins**   **Cook Time: 30mins.**

Calories: 216   **Protein: 33.2g**   **Carbs: 0.5g**   **Fat: 8.8g**

Cumin-Spiced Lamb Chops

Ingredients

- 4 lamb chops
- 2 cloves garlic, mashed
- 2 teaspoons whole cumin seeds
- 2 teaspoons red pepper flakes
- 2 teaspoons coarse sea salt
- 2 teaspoons coarse pepper
- 1 tablespoon olive oil

Directions

Preheat the water bath to 140 degrees F. Rub the lamb chops with salt, pepper, garlic, cumin, and red pepper. Seal into the bag. Place in water bath and cook 2-4 hours. Remove lamb from bag and pat dry. Sear on a boiling pan with olive oil until brown on both sides.

Serves: 2   **Prep Time: 20mins**   **Cook Time: 4hr. 20min**

Calories: 200   **Protein: 17.68g**   **Carbs: 3.96g**
    Fat: 13.12g

Beef Wellington

Ingredients:

- ½ beef tenderloin, unsliced, silver skin removed
- 1 teaspoon salt
- 1 teaspoon pepper
- ¼ pound prosciutto, sliced thin
- ½ cup mushrooms, minced
- 1 shallot, minced
- ½ tablespoon tomato paste
- 2 tablespoons butter, softened
- 1 sheet refrigerated puff pastry
- 1 egg, beaten

Directions

Preheat the sous vide bath to 140 degrees F. Season the beef to taste then add to a vacuum seal bag. Seal, and cook in bath for about an hour. Set in the refrigerator. Sauté shallots in butter until translucent, then add mushrooms and sauté until cooked. Pour into a bowl and stir in tomato paste.

When the beef has cooled completely, preheat oven to 400 degrees F. Lay puff pastry on a cutting board and spread a layer of prosciutto on top.

Place the chilled beef on top of the puff pastry and spread the duxelles on all sides of the beef. Wrap the prosciutto-lined pastry around the beef and seal with egg. Brush remaining egg over pastry to glaze.

Bake beef Wellington 15 minutes or until puff pastry is golden-brown and fully cooked. Slice across the grain to serve.

Serves: 6   **Prep Time: 40mins**   **Cook Time: 1hr. 15min**

Calories: 649   **Protein: 40.48g**   **Carbs: 5.49g**   **Fat: 13.01g**

Sunday Roast

Ingredients:

- 3lbs. chuck roast
- 2 tablespoons coarse salt
- 1 tablespoon coarse pepper
- 1 large sprig fresh rosemary
- 1 tablespoon olive oil

Directions

Preheat the water bath to 140 degrees F. Season the beef with salt and pepper. Seal it into a bag with the rosemary. Place in water bath and cook 24 hours.

After 24 hours, remove beef from bag and pat dry. Sear in olive oil in a hot pan until brown on all sides.

Serves: 6 20min   **Prep Time: 20mins**   **Cook Time: 24hr.**

Calories: 305   **Protein: 46.75g**   **Carbs: 0.74g**
      Fat: 13.01g

Rolled Beef

Ingredients:

Beef:

- 8 4oz. sliced beef
- Salt and pepper, to taste
- ¼ cup vegetable oil, to fry

Filling:

- 4oz. peas
- 1 sprig thyme
- 1 pinch sugar
- 4oz. carrots, chopped
- 8 teaspoon Dijon mustard
- 16 slices bacon

Directions:

Preheat Sous Vide cooker to 176 degrees F. Place the peas in a Sous Vide bag. Add the carrots, a pinch of sugar and salt to taste. Vacuum seal the bag and place in a water bath. Cook the veggies 30 minutes. Remove from the bag.

Cover the beef slices with parchment paper. Pound with a meat tenderizer to make the beef this. Spread the mustard over meat, and top each slice with two pieces bacon. Roll the meat into roulade, then roll the meat over veggies and secure the roulades with a kitchen twine. Season with salt and pepper. Heat the oil in a skillet and sear the roulades on all sides. Cool the roulades and transfer in a Sous Vide bag. Vacuum seal the beef and cook 37 hours at 153 degrees F.

Remove the meat from the cooker. Allow cooling completely before removing from the bag. Remove the kitchen twine and slice before serving.

Serves: 8   **Prep Time: 30mins**   **Cook Time: 37 hrs.**

Calories: 287   **Protein: 15.2g**   **Carbs: 4.4g**   **Fat: 23g**

Short Ribs Provençale

Ingredients

- 2 lbs. beef short ribs
- 1 teaspoon salt
- 1 teaspoon pepper
- 3 cloves garlic
- 2 sprigs fresh thyme
- 1 sprig fresh rosemary
- 2 bay leaves
- 1 tablespoon butter
- 1 tablespoon olive oil
- 1 tablespoon flour
- 2 cups red wine
- 2 cups beef stock
- 1 tablespoon tomato paste
- Crusty bread for serving

Directions

Preheat the water bath to 140 degrees F. Season the beef liberally with salt and pepper. Place in bag with garlic, thyme, rosemary, and bay leaves. Seal and place in water bath. Cook 48 hours. 48 hours later, prepare the sauce. Remove the beef from the bag and pat dry. In a Dutch oven or heavy-bottomed pan, melt butter with olive oil. Add beef and sear until brown on all sides. Remove beef to a plate.

Stir flour into the pan and cook 30 seconds, then deglaze with wine, stirring rapidly and scraping the bottom. Stir in beef stock, tomato paste, and any liquid that collected in the sous vide bag. Reduce sauce to your desired consistency. Serve over short ribs.

Serves: 4   **Prep Time: 30mins**   **Cook Time: 48hrs. 30min**

Calories: 551   **Protein: 48.73g**   **Carbs: 7.87g**   **Fat: 26.82g**

Simple Spiced Ribs

Ingredients

- 1.5 lb. baby back ribs
- 1 tablespoon fine salt
- 1 tablespoon brown sugar
- 1 tablespoon smoked paprika
- ½ tablespoon ground cumin
- ½ tablespoon ground coriander
- ½ tablespoon black pepper
- ¼ tablespoon dried garlic
- 1 tablespoon dried parsley
- ½ cup BBQ sauce

Directions

Preheat Sous-vide cooker to 155 degrees F. Combine all the spices and parsley in a bowl. Rub the ribs with this dry mixture. Place the ribs in a Sous Vide bag and submerge in water. Cook the ribs 24 hours.

Remove the ribs from the bag. Preheat your grill. Cook the ribs 7-8 minutes, basting with BBQ sauce all the way. Serve while hot with fresh salad.

Serves: 4   **Prep Time: 10mins**   **Cook Time: 24hrs.**

Calories: 446   **Protein: 45.3g**   **Carbs: 15.6g**   **Fat: 21.3g**

Spiced Beef Brisket

Ingredients:

- 2lb. beef brisket
- Salt and pepper, to taste
- 2 tablespoons olive oil
- ½ tablespoon tomato paste
- 4 cloves garlic, minced
- 1 tablespoon smoked paprika
- ½ tablespoon beef demi-glace
- 1 teaspoon chopped thyme
- 1 cup beef stock
- ½ cup red wine
- 2 tablespoons honey
- ¾ lb. carrots, peeled, cut into matchsticks

Directions:

Preheat your Sous Vide cooker to 155 degrees F. Season the brisket with salt and pepper. Place the brisket into Sous Vide cooking bag. Place aside. Heat ½ tablespoon olive oil in a saucepan. Add tomato paste, garlic, smoked paprika, demi-glace, thyme, stock, and wine. Simmer 5 minutes.

Stir in the honey and season to taste. Simmer 1 minute. Pour the mixture into the bag with beef and vacuum seal the bag. Carefully place the bag into the cooker and cook 32 hours.

25 minutes before the beef is done, toss the carrots with 1 tablespoon olive oil.

Roast the carrots 20-25 minutes at 450 degrees F. Remove the bag from cooker and open carefully. Strain the sauce into a small saucepot. Simmer 3 minutes over medium heat. Heat the remaining olive oil in a large skillet. Sear the beef 3 minutes per side. Serve the beef with roasted carrots and prepared sauce.

Serves: 4   **Prep Time: 20mins**   **Cook Time: 32hrs.**

Calories: 309   **Protein: 18.3g**   **Carbs: 20.4g**   **Fat: 15.4g**

Pork

BLT

Ingredients

- 1 package thick-cut bacon in original vacuum-sealed packaging
- 6 slices bread, toasted
- 6 slices tomato
- 3 leaves lettuce
- 3 tablespoons mayonnaise

Directions

Preheat the water bath to 140 degrees F. Place sealed bacon in the water bath. Cook at least 4 hours or overnight. After at least 4 hours, remove bacon from pan. Brown in the hot pan on both sides. Drain on paper towel. Spread mayonnaise on bread. Assemble sandwiches with tomato and lettuce. Serve.

Serves: 3　　**Prep Time: 20mins**　　**Cook Time: 4 hrs. 20 min**

Calories: 812　**Protein: 22.74g**　　**Carbs: 22.56g Fat: 70.07g**

Pulled Pork

Ingredients:

- 2lb. pork shoulder, trimmed
- 1 tablespoon ketchup
- 4 tablespoons Dijon mustard
- 2 tablespoons maple syrup
- 2 tablespoons soy sauce

Directions:

Preheat your Sous Vide cooker to 158 degrees F. In a bowl, combine ketchup, mustard, maple syrup, and soy sauce. Place the pork with prepared sauce into Sous Vide bag. Vacuum seal the bag and submerge in water. Cook the pork 24 hours.

Open the bag and remove pork. Strain cooking juices into a saucepan. Torch the pork to create a crust. Simmer the cooking juices in a saucepan until thickened.

Pull pork before serving. Serve with thickened sauce.

Serves: 6 **Prep Time: 10mins** **Cook Time: 24 hrs.**

Calories: 471 **Protein: 36g** **Carbs: 6.1g** **Fat: 32.8g**

Barbecue Ribs

Ingredients

- 1 rack pork ribs
- 1 tablespoon salt
- 1 teaspoon pepper
- 2 tablespoons brown sugar
- 1 tablespoon garlic powder
- 1 tablespoon onion powder
- 2 tablespoons paprika
- ½ cup barbecue sauce, plus extra for serving

Directions

Preheat the water bath to 165 degrees F. Combine salt, pepper, sugar, garlic powder, onion powder, and paprika. Rub all over ribs. Seal ribs into bag and place in water bath. Cook 12 hours.

When ribs are cooked, place on a baking sheet lined with aluminum foil. Spread barbecue sauce over ribs. Place under broiler until sauce bubbles. Serve with additional sauce.

Serves: 4   **Prep Time:** 20mins   **Cook Time:** 12 hrs.

Calories: 579   **Protein:** 72.06g   **Carbs:** 23.99g   **Fat:** 19.91g

Indian Style Pork

Ingredients

- 1.5lb. pork tenderloin, sliced
- 2 cups yogurt
- 1 cup sour cream
- 2 tablespoons tandoori paste
- 1 tablespoon curry paste
- 1-inch ginger, minced
- 2 cloves garlic, minced
- Salt and pepper, to taste

Directions

In a large bowl, combine yogurt, sour cream, tandoori paste, curry paste, garlic, and ginger. Add sliced pork. Cover and marinate 20 minutes in a fridge. Preheat your Sous Vide cooker to 135 degrees F. Remove the pork from marinade and place into Sous Vide bag. Vacuum seal the bag. Submerge pork in the water bath and cook 2 hours.

Remove the bag from water and open carefully. Heat 1 tablespoon olive oil in a large skillet. Sear the pork 3 minutes per side. Serve warm.

Serves: 4   **Prep Time: 15mins**   **Cook Time: 2 hrs.**

Calories: 363   Protein: 12.74g   Carbs: 13.1g   Fat: 19.5g

Breakfast Sausage Patties

Ingredients:

- 1 lb. ground pork
- 1 teaspoon salt
- ½ teaspoon pepper
- 1 clove garlic, minced
- ½ onion, minced
- ½ teaspoon dried thyme
- ½ teaspoon dried rosemary
- ½ teaspoon dried sage
- ½ teaspoon dried parsley
- 1 egg
- 1 tablespoon olive oil

Directions

Preheat the water bath to 140 degrees F. Mash together all ingredients in a bowl. Place in bag and press to fill all corners in a flat patty. Seal bag, place in the water bath and cook 2 hours. When pork is cooked, cut off the bag. Cut patty into squares. Immediately before serving, heat oil in a pan. Sear patties in oil until brown on both sides. Serve.

Serves: 4   **Prep Time: 20mins**   **Cook Time: 20 hrs. 20 min**

Calories: 407   **Protein: 34.64g**   **Carbs: 2.14g   Fat: 29.39g**

Pork Medallions

Ingredients

- 1 tablespoon olive oil
- 1 pinch salt
- 1 pinch black pepper
- 1 teaspoon ground cumin
- ¼ cup chopped fresh parsley
- 1 ¾ lb. pork tenderloin

Directions

Preheat the Sous Vide cooker to 145 degrees F. Cut the pork tenderloin in medallions. Season with salt, pepper, and cumin. Place the seasoned pork into Sous Vide bag and add parsley. Vacuum seals the bag and submerge in water.

Cook the medallions 1 hour.

Heat olive oil in a large skillet. Remove the medallions from the cooker.

Sear on both sides. Serve warm.

Serves: 4   **Prep Time: 10mins**   **Cook Time: 1 hr.**

Calories: 317   **Protein: 52.1g**   **Carbs: 0.5g**   **Fat: 10.6g**

Pork Osso Bucco

Ingredients

- 2 pork shanks
- 1 tablespoon olive oil
- ½ sweet onion, finely chopped
- 1 carrot, finely chopped
- 1 stalk celery, finely chopped
- 4 cloves garlic, minced
- 1 teaspoon salt
- 1 teaspoon pepper
- ½ cup white wine
- 7 oz. whole tomatoes, crushed
- 2 bay leaves
- 2 sprigs rosemary
- 2 sprigs thyme
- Crusty bread for serving

Directions

Preheat the water bath to 175 degrees F. Meanwhile, prepare the sauce. Heat 1 tablespoon olive oil in a saucepan. Add onions, carrots, and celery and cook until onion is translucent. Add garlic and stir. Pour in wine and tomatoes and cook until sauce is reduced and alcohol smell has evaporated. Remove from heat.

Season the shanks with salt and pepper. Place each shank into a separate bag and add half the sauce to each bag. Divide the herbs between the bags. Seal and place into the water bath. Cook 24 hours. Serve with crusty bread.

Serves: 2 **Prep Time: 30mins** **Cook Time: 24 hrs.**

Calories: 683 **Protein: 102.2g** **Carbs: 18.25g** **Fat: 20.71g**

Pork Knuckles

Ingredients:

- 2 10oz. pork knuckles
- Salt and pepper, to taste
- 4 cloves garlic, chopped
- ½ cup mustard
- ½ cup raw apple cider vinegar
- 2 ¾ cups apple juice
- ½ cup brown sugar
- 4 sprigs thyme
- 1 bay leaf

Directions

Preheat Sous Vide cooker to 158 degrees F. Generously season pork knuckles with salt and pepper. Heat some oil in a large skillet. Sear pork 2 minutes per side. Remove from the skillet. Toss the remaining ingredients into a skillet, and cook until reduced by half. Place aside to cool. Place the pork knuckles in Sous Vide bag along with the prepared sauce. Vacuum seal the bag. Submerge bag in a water bath. Cook 24 hours.

Remove shanks from the bag and place aside. Strain cooking juices into a saucepan. Simmer over medium heat until thickened. Pour the sauce over shanks and serve.

Serves: 4   **Prep Time: 20mins**   **Cook Time: 24 hrs.**

Calories: 358   **Protein: 24.9g**   **Carbs: 45.2g**   **Fat: 8.6g**

Carnitas Tacos

Ingredients

- 2 lbs. pork shoulder
- 1 teaspoon salt
- 1 teaspoon pepper
- 1 onion, chopped
- 3 cloves garlic
- ½ teaspoon ground cumin
- 2 bay leaves
- Corn tortillas for serving
- Fresh cilantro for serving
- Lime for serving

Directions

Preheat the water bath to 185 degrees F. Rub pork with salt, pepper, and cumin. Seal into the bag with onion, garlic, and bay leaves. Place into the water bath and cook 16 hours.

When pork is cooked, remove from bag and shred with two forks or your hands. To serve, place a small amount of pork in a tortilla and top with cilantro and a squeeze of lime.

Serves: 4   **Prep Time: 30mins**   **Cook Time: 16 hrs.**

Calories: 623   **Protein: 57.43g**   **Carbs: 3.9g**   **Fat: 40.24g**

Tokyo-Style Pork Ramen

Ingredients

- ½ pound pork belly
- ¼ cup brown sugar
- ¼ cup soy sauce
- ¼ cup dry sherry

For soup:

- 3 cups chicken broth
- 1 teaspoon sugar
- 1 tablespoon dry sherry
- 3 tablespoons soy sauce
- 2 packages fresh ramen noodles
- 2 scallions, sliced

Directions

Preheat the water bath to 170°F. Combine sugar, soy sauce, and sherry. Spread over pork. Seal into bag, place in the water bath, and cook 10 hours. ½ hour before pork is cooked, prepare the soup. In a pot, combine chicken broth, sugar, sherry, and soy sauce. Season to taste. Cook ramen noodles according to package instructions. Divide noodles and broth between two bowls. When pork is cooked, slice into ½-inch thick pieces. Divide between bowls of ramen and top with scallion.

Serves: 2   **Prep Time: 30mins**   **Cook Time: 10 hrs.**

Calories: 1140   **Protein: 26.1g**   **Carbs: 83.19g**   **Fat: 75.48g**

Fish & Seafood

Whole Red Snapper

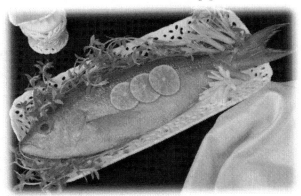

Ingredients

- 1 small red snapper, cleaned and gutted
- 1 teaspoon salt
- 1 teaspoon pepper
- 4 garlic cloves, crushed
- 2 sprigs rosemary
- 1 lemon, cut into wedges
- 2 tablespoons butter, cut into cubes

Directions

Preheat the water bath to 140 degrees F. Season the fish all over with salt and pepper. Stuff the center of the fish with garlic, rosemary, half the lemon, and butter. Seal into a bag and place in water bath. Cook 60 minutes. Serve with remaining lemon wedges.

Serves: 2 **Prep Time: 20mins** **Cook Time: 1 hr.**

Calories: 800 **Protein: 140.29g** **Carbs: 4.58g** **Fat: 20.77g**

Coriander Garlic Squids

Ingredients

- 4 4oz. squids, cleaned
- ¼ cup olive oil
- ¼ cup chopped coriander
- 4 cloves garlic, minced
- 2 chili peppers, chopped
- 2 teaspoons minced ginger
- ¼ cup vegetable oil
- 1 lemon, cut into wedges
- Salt and pepper, to taste

Directions

Set the Sous vide cooker to 136 degrees F. Place the squids and 2 tablespoons olive oil in a Sous Vide bags. Season to taste and vacuum seal the bag.

Submerge in water and cook 2 hours.

Heat remaining olive oil in a skillet. Add garlic, chili pepper, and ginger and cook 1 minute. Add half the coriander and stir well. Remove from the heat. Remove the squids from the bag. Heat vegetable oil in a skillet, until sizzling hot. Add the squid and cook 30 seconds per side. Transfer the squids onto a plate. Top with garlic-coriander mixture and sprinkle with the remaining coriander. Serve with lemon.

Serves: 4   **Prep Time: 20min**   **Cook Time: 2 hrs.**

Calories: 346   **Protein: 18.2g**   **Carbs: 6.7g**   **Fat: 18.56g**

Lazy Man's Lobster

Ingredients:

- Tail and claws of 1 lobster
- 2 tablespoons butter
- 1 clove garlic, minced
- ½ tablespoon fresh thyme, minced
- ¼ cup sherry
- ½ teaspoon salt
- ½ teaspoon pepper
- ¼ cup heavy cream
- Toast for serving

Directions

Preheat the water bath to 140°F. Seal lobster into the bag. Place in water bath and cook 1 hour. Meanwhile, prepare the sauce. Melt butter in a pan. Add garlic and thyme and cook 30 seconds. Add sherry and bring to a boil. Remove from heat and stir in cream. Season with salt and pepper. When lobster is cooked, remove the shell and stir into sauce. Serve with toast.

Serves: 1   **Prep Time:** 20mins   **Cook Time:** 1 hr.

Calories: 582   **Protein:** 26.7g   **Carbs:** 5.45g   **Fat:** 46.26g

Salmon with Yogurt Dill Sauce

Ingredients

- 2 salmon fillets
- ½ teaspoon salt
- ½ teaspoon pepper
- 2-4 sprigs fresh dill

For sauce:

- 1 cup plain Greek yogurt
- 1 tablespoon fresh dill, minced
- Juice of 1 lemon
- ½ teaspoon salt
- ½ teaspoon pepper

Directions

Season salmon with salt and pepper. Seal into the bag with dill. Refrigerate ½ hour. Preheat the water bath to 140 degrees F. Place salmon into the water bath and cook 20 minutes. Meanwhile, prepare the sauce. Combine all sauce ingredients and season to taste. When salmon is cooked, arrange on a plate and top with sauce.

Serves: 2 **Prep Time:** 10hrs. **Cook Time:** 20min

Calories: 498 **Protein:** 70.12g **Carbs:** 10.16g **Fat:** 18.56g

Crab Zucchini Roulade & Mousse

Ingredients

- 3lb. crab legs and claws
- 2 tablespoons olive oil
- 1 medium zucchini
- Salt and pepper, to taste

Mousse:

- 1 avocado, peeled, pitted
- 1 tablespoon Worcestershire sauce
- 2 tablespoons crème Fraiche
- 2 tablespoons fresh lime juice
- Salt, to taste

Directions:

Preheat Sous vide cooker to 185F. Place the claws and legs in a Sous Vide bag and vacuum seal. Submerge the bag with content in a water bath. Cook the crab 10 minutes. Slice the zucchini with a vegetable peeler. This way you will have some skinny strips.

Remove the crab from the water bath and crack the shell. Flake the meat and transfer into a bowl. Add olive oil, salt, and pepper, and stir to bind gently. Make the mousse; in a food blender, blend the avocado and crème Fraiche until smooth. Stir in the remaining ingredients and spoon the mixture into piping bag. Arrange the zucchini slices on aluminum foil and fill with the crab meat. Roll up the zucchinis and crab into a log and refrigerate 30 minutes. To serve; cut the roulade into four pieces. Serve onto a plate with some avocado mousse. Enjoy.

Serves: 4   **Prep Time: 30mins**   **Cook Time: 10min**

Calories: 415   **Protein: 49.3g**   **Carbs: 1.6g**   **Fat: 35.5g**

Sole Fish & Bacon

Ingredients:

- 10oz. sole fish fillets
- 2 tablespoons olive oil
- 2 slices bacon
- ½ tablespoon lemon juice
- Salt and pepper, to taste

Directions:

Preheat Sous Vide cooker to 132 degrees F. Cook the bacon in a non-stick skillet and cook bacon until crispy. Remove the bacon and place aside. Season fish fillets with salt, pepper, and lemon juice. Brush the fish with olive oil. Place the fish in a Sous Vide bag. Top the fish with the bacon. Vacuum seal the bag. Submerge in a water bath and cook 25 minutes. Remove the fish from the bag. Serve while warm.

Serves: 2 **Prep Time: 10mins** **Cook Time: 25mins**

Calories: 298 **Protein: 22.4g** **Carbs: 0.4g** **Fat: 22.9g**

Crusted Tuna Fish

Ingredients:

- 3 tablespoons all-purpose flour
- 3 tablespoons ground almonds
- ½ tablespoon butter
- 4 5oz. tuna fillets

Marinade:

- 1 pinch chili powder
- 1 pinch salt
- 1 pinch black pepper
- 5 tablespoons vegetable oil
- 2 teaspoons lemon juice

Directions:

Preheat Sous Vide cooker to 132 degrees F. Combine the marinade ingredients in a Sous Vide bag. Add the tuna and vacuum seal. Submerge in a water bath and cook 25 minutes.

Remove the fish from Sous vide bag. Pat dry the fish. In a bowl, combine all-purpose flour and almonds. Sprinkle with a pinch of salt. Heat the butter in a large skillet. Coat the tuna with the flour-nut mixture and fry in butter until golden brown. Serve warm.

Serves: 4   **Prep Time: 10mins**   **Cook Time: 25mins**

Calories: 324   **Protein: 39.2g**   **Carbs: 5.4g**   **Fat: 15.2g**

Teriyaki Salmon

Ingredients

- 1-inch fresh ginger, peeled and sliced
- 10 oz. skinless salmon fillets
- 4 oz. egg noodles
- 1 tablespoon sesame oil
- ½ cup + 1 teaspoon teriyaki sauce
- 1 tablespoon sesame seeds, toasted
- 2 teaspoons soy sauce
- 2 teaspoons thinly sliced scallions
- 4 oz. lettuce, chopped
- 1/8 small red onion, sliced thinly
- 1 tablespoon roasted sesame dressing

Directions

Add a half of your teriyaki sauce evenly to 2 vacuum pack bags with your salmon, seal, and set to marinate in the refrigerator for about 15 minutes.

Set the Sous Vide cooker to preheat to 131F. Add your vacuum bags in the bath and allow to cook for about 15 minutes. Cook egg noodles using the directions on the package Drain well, return to cooking pot and stir in sesame oil and soy sauce, reserving one teaspoon. Divide pasta between serving plates.

Combine the other half of teriyaki sauce, ginger, soy sauce, and scallions to a small bowl and stir to combine. Combine onion and lettuce then drizzle with a teaspoon of roasted sesame dressing.

When the timer goes off, remove salmon from the water bath, reserving cooking liquid. Top the pasta with salmon fillets and drizzle all with reserved cooking liquid. Garnish salmon with sesame seeds and serve with prepared salad and dipping sauce.

Serves: 2 **Prep Time: 10mins** **Cook Time: 15mins**

Calories: 291 **Protein: 33g** **Carbs: 15.2g** **Fat: 11.2g**

Swordfish Piccata

Ingredients:

- 2 swordfish steaks
- 1 teaspoon salt
- 1 teaspoon pepper
- 2 tablespoons olive oil
- ¼ cup butter
- 2 cloves garlic, minced
- 2 tablespoons lemon juice
- 2 tablespoons capers, with juice
- 2 tablespoons fresh basil, chopped

Directions

Set the sous vide machine to preheat to 140°F. Season swordfish to taste, then seal into a vacuum pack bag. Place in water bath and cook 30 minutes. Meanwhile, prepare the sauce. Melt butter with olive oil. Add garlic and cook 30 seconds. Stir in lemon juice and capers with juice, then add basil. When swordfish is cooked, transfer to plate. Serve topped with sauce.

Serves: 2   **Prep Time:** 20mins   **Cook Time:** 30mins

Calories: 623   **Protein:** 39.94g   **Carbs:** 3.48g   **Fat:** 49.92g

Sous Vide Lobster

Ingredients

- 1lb. lobster tail, cleaned
- ¾ cup butter, cubed
- 2 sprigs tarragon
- 1 lime, cut into wedges
- Salt, to taste

Directions

Preheat Sous Vide cooker to 134 degrees F. In a Sous Vide bag, combine lobster tail, cubed butter, tarragon, and salt. Vacuum seal the bag. Submerge the bag in a water bath and cook 1 hour.

Remove the bag from the water bath. Open carefully, and transfer the lobster onto a plate. Drizzle the lobster tail with cooking/butter sauce. Serve with lime wedges.

Serves: 4   Prep Time: 10mins   Cook Time: 1 hr.

Calories: 412   Protein: 22.1g   Carbs: 2g   Fat: 35.5g

Basics, Sauces, and Marinades

Sweet and Sour Sauce

Ingredients

- 1/3 cup olive oil
- 1 shallot, chopped
- 1 cup fresh pineapple chunks
- ¼ cup rice vinegar
- Salt and pepper, to taste

Directions

Preheat Sous Vide cooker to 130F. Combine all ingredients in a Sous Vide bag. Seal the bag using immersion water technique. Cook the pineapple 2 hours.

Remove the bag from the cooker. Open the bag and allow to cool 10 minutes.

Transfer the pineapple, and cooking juices into a food blender. Blend until smooth. Serve.

Serves: 6 **Prep Time: 10mins** **Cook Time: 2 hrs.**

Calories: 118 **Protein: 0.2g** **Carbs: 3.9g** **Fat: 11.2g**

Hollandaise Sauce

Ingredients

- 1 ½ cups butter
- 4 egg yolks
- ½ cup water
- 2 ½ tablespoons white wine vinegar
- 1 teaspoon salt

Directions

Preheat Sous Vide cooker to 167F. Whisk all ingredients in a bowl.

Pour the sauce into Sous Vide bag and seal the bag using water immersion technique. Submerge sauce in water and cook 30 minutes.

Remove the bag from the cooker. Open the bag and transfer the bag content into a bowl. Whisk 30 seconds using an electric whisk. Serve.

Serves: 8　　　　**Prep Time:** 5mins　　　　**Cook Time:** 30mins

Calories: 332　　**Protein:** 1.7g　　　**Carbs:** 0.3g　　**Fat:** 36.8g

Tomato Sauce

Ingredients

- 2 tablespoons olive oil
- 2 onions, chopped
- 2 cloves garlic, minced
- 2lb. cherry tomatoes
- 2 sprigs fresh basil
- 3 sprigs fresh oregano
- 1/3 cup fresh chopped parsley
- Salt, to taste

Directions

Preheat Sous vide cooker to 180F. Heat olive oil in a skillet. Add onions and cook 5 minutes. Toss in the garlic and cook 30 seconds. Insert the tomatoes and stir to coat with oil. Place aside to cool. Transfer the tomatoes in Sous Vide bag. Add the remaining ingredients and seal using water immersion technique. Cook the tomatoes 50 minutes.

Remove the bag from the cooker. Open the bag and chill 15 minutes. Peel the tomatoes and place in a food blender, with cooking juices. Discard the herbs. Blend the tomatoes until smooth. Serve or use later.

Serves: 12   **Prep Time:** 10mins   **Cook Time:** 50mins

Calories: 42   **Protein:** 1g   **Carbs:** 4.9g   **Fat:** 2.5g

Cranberry Sauce

Ingredients

- 3 cups cranberries
- ½ cup sugar
- ½ orange, zested

Directions

Preheat Sous Vide cooker to 180F. Combine all ingredients in a Sous Vide bag. Vacuum seal the bag and cook the cranberries 2 hours.

Remove the bag from the cooker. Leave the cranberries to cool completely in a bag. Once cooled, transfer to a serving bowl.

Serves: 6 **Prep Time: 10mins** **Cook Time: 2 hrs.**

Calories: 100 **Protein: 0.1g** **Carbs: 23.5g** **Fat: 0g**

Béarnaise Sauce

Ingredients

- ¼ cup white wine
- 2 sprigs fresh tarragon
- 1 shallot, minced
- 2 egg yolks
- ¼ cup butter
- ½ teaspoon salt
- ½ teaspoon pepper

Directions

Preheat the water bath to 170°F.

Combine all ingredients in a bag and seal. Place in water bath and cook 1 hour.

Remove tarragon sprigs. Blend until smooth.

Serves: 2 **Prep Time:** 20mins **Cook Time:** 1 hr.

Calories: 288   **Protein:** 3.16g   **Carbs:** 3.9g   **Fat:** 27.58g

Creme Anglaise

Ingredients

- 3 egg yolks
- ½ cup milk
- ¼ cup heavy cream
- ¼ cup sugar
- 1 teaspoon vanilla

Directions

1. Preheat the water bath to 170°F.
2. Combine all ingredients in a bag. Seal and cook 20 minutes.
3. Blend sauce until smooth. Transfer to refrigerator and cool completely before serving.

Serves: 2　　　　　**Prep Time: 20mins**　　　　**Cook Time: 20mins**

Calories: 277　　**Protein: 6.58g**　　　**Carbs: 17.4g**　**Fat: 19.7g**

Basil Tomato Sauce

Ingredients:

- 1 can (28-ounce) whole tomatoes, crushed
- 1 onion, diced
- 2 cloves garlic, minced
- 1 tablespoon olive oil
- 1 bay leaf
- 1 sprig rosemary
- ½ teaspoon salt
- ½ teaspoon pepper
- 1 cup fresh basil, chopped
- Cooked pasta for serving

Directions

Preheat the water bath to 185°F.

Combine all ingredients in a bag. Seal and place in water bath. Cook 1 hour.

Remove bay leaves and rosemary sprig. Serve with cooked pasta.

Serves: 2   **Prep Time: 20mins**   **Cook Time: 1 hr**

Calories: 158   **Protein: 4.57g**   **Carbs: 21.4g**   **Fat: 7.9.g**

Hot Sauce

Ingredients

- 1 ½ lb. jalapenos, seeded and chopped
- 1/3 cup rice wine vinegar
- 6 cloves garlic, minced
- 3 tablespoons light honey
- 1 teaspoon fine salt

Directions

Preheat Sous Vide cooker to 210F. Combine jalapenos, garlic, and salt into Sous vide bag. Seal the bag using water immersion technique. Submerge the bag into a water bath and cook 25 minutes.

Remove the bag from the water bath and pour the content into a bowl. Stir in the vinegar and honey. Serve or store in a fridge.

Serves: 10 **Prep Time: 5mins** **Cook Time: 25mins**

Calories: 28 **Protein: 1g** **Carbs: 4.6g** **Fat: 0.4g**

Applesauce

Ingredients

- 3 apples, coarsely chopped
- 1 cinnamon stick

Directions

1. Preheat the water bath to 170°F.
2. Seal all ingredients in the bag. Cook 3 hours.
3. Transfer apples to a bowl. Remove cinnamon stick. Mash to your desired consistency.

Serves: 2 **Prep Time: 30mins** **Cook Time: 3hrs**

Calories: 142 **Protein: 0.7g** **Carbs: 37.7g** **Fat: 0.46g**

Soy Chili Sauce

Ingredients

- 1 cup light soy sauce
- 2 green chilies, chopped, seeded
- ¼ cup honey
- 1 teaspoon cumin

Directions

Preheat Sous Vide cooker to 160F. Combine all ingredients in Sous Vide bag. Seal using water immersion technique. Submerge the bag into the water bath.

Cook 30 minutes.

Remove the bag from cooker and serve sauce in a bowl.

Serves: 8 **Prep Time:** 5mins **Cook Time:** 30mins

Calories: 35 **Protein:** 0.5g **Carbs:** 10.8g **Fat:** 0.1g

DRINKS, DESSERTS, AND FRUITS

Rummy Eggnog

Ingredients

- 4 eggs
- 2 cups whole milk
- 1 cup heavy cream
- ½ tablespoon vanilla
- ¾ cup sugar
- 2 cinnamon sticks
- ½ cup rum
- Freshly-grated nutmeg for garnish

Directions

Preheat the water bath to 140°F. Beat eggs until pale and fluffy. Beat in milk, cream, vanilla, and sugar. Pour into bag with the cinnamon stick and seal using water immersion method. Place bag in water bath and cook 1 hour.

Strain solids from the bag using a coffee filter or cheesecloth. Chill completely.

To serve, pour into glasses and top with freshly-grated nutmeg.

Serves: 4 **Prep Time: 30mins** **Cook Time: 1 hr**

Calories: 551 **Protein: 14g** **Carbs: 27.4g** **Fat: 35.54g**

"Barrel-Aged" Negroni

Ingredients

- ½ cup gin
- ½ cup vermouth
- ½ cup Campari
- ½ cup water
- 1 orange, cut into wedges
- ½ cup winemaking toasted oak chips

Directions

1. Preheat the water bath to 120°F.
2. Combine all ingredients in a bag. Seal and place in water bath. Cook 24 hours.
3. Strain solids from liquid using a coffee filter or cheesecloth. Serve over ice.

Serves: 4   Prep Time: 20mins   Cook Time: 20mins

Calories: 216   Protein: 0.07g   Carbs: 17.3g   Fat: 0.07g

Strawberry Ice Cream

Ingredients:

- 2 cups strawberries
- ½ cup fine sugar
- 1 cup heavy cream
- 1 cup milk
- 5 egg yolks
- ½ cup granulated sugar
- 1 teaspoon vanilla paste

Directions:

Set the sous vide cooker to preheat to 180 degrees F. Add sugar and strawberries to a vacuum pack bag. Seal, and set to cook in the bath for about 30 minutes. Remove the bag from the cooker and strain the strawberries through the fine mesh sieve, pressing to remove pulp. Discard the seeds. Combine heavy cream, milk, egg yolks, granulated sugar, and vanilla paste in a food blender. Blend until smooth. Stir in the strawberry mixture and transfer all into a large bag.

Seal the bag using water immersion technique and cook in Sous Vide cooker for 1 hour. When the timer goes off, remove the bag from the cooker and lace into ice-cold water bath 30 minutes. Churn the mixture into an ice cream machine until set. Serve.

Serves: 6   **Prep Time: 30mins**   **Cook Time: 1 hr 30min**

Calories: 218   **Protein: 4.5g**   **Carbs: 24.6g**   **Fat: 12.3g**

Lime-Ginger Gin Tonic

Ingredients

- 1 cup gin
- 1 lime, cut into wedges
- 1-inch ginger, peeled
- 1 ¼ cup tonic water
- 1 cup ice

Directions

1. Preheat the water bath to 125°F.
2. Pour gin, ginger, and half the lime into a bag. Seal and place in water bath. Cook 2 hours. After 2 hours, remove to the refrigerator and cool completely.
3. When gin infusion is cool, divide ice between 4 glasses. Strain solids from the gin. Pour an equal amount of the gin infusion into each glass. Garnish with lime wedge.

Serves: 4   Prep Time: 20mins   Cook Time: 2 hrs.

Calories: 630   Protein: 0.22g   Carbs: 30.9g   Fat: 0.05g

Mocha Coffee Liqueur

Ingredients

- 1 ½ cups vodka
- 1 lb. coffee beans
- ½ cup cacao nibs
- 1 cup sugar
- 1 vanilla bean, split

Directions

Preheat sous vide to 150°F.

Combine all ingredients in a bag and seal. Place in water bath and cook 24 hours.

Strain solids from the bag using a coffee filter or cheesecloth. Transfer to a bottle and bring to room temperature before using in your favorite cocktails.

Serves: 8   **Prep Time:** 20mins   **Cook Time:** 24 hrs

Calories: 244   **Protein:** 1.7g   **Carbs:** 21.49g   **Fat:** 6.3g

Tom Collins Cocktail

Ingredients

- 7 cups gin
- 1 cup lemon juice
- 2 cups lemon rind
- 1 ½ cups granulated sugar
- Soda water, to serve with

Directions

Preheat Sous Vide to 131F. In a large Sous vide bag, combine gin, lemon juice, lemon rind, and sugar. Fold the edges of the bag few times and clip to the side of your pot. Cook the cocktail 1 hour.

Strain the cocktail into a large glass jug. Place aside to cool completely before use.

Serve over ice, and finish off with soda water. Garnish the cocktail with lemon rind or fresh thyme.

Serves: 20   **Prep Time: 10mins**   **Cook Time: 1 hr**

Calories: 270   **Protein: 0.3g**   **Carbs: 17.2g**   **Fat: 0.2g**

Cherry Manhattan

Ingredients

- Bourbon infusion:
- 2 cups bourbon
- ¼ cup raw cacao nibs
- 1 cup dried cherries

To finish:

- 4oz. sweet vermouth
- 1 Chocolate bitters, as desired

Directions

Make the infusion; preheat Sous Vide to 122F. In a Sous Vide bag combine bourbon, cacao nibs, and cherries. Seal the bag, and cook 1 hour

Remove the bag from the water bath and let cool. Strain the content into a jar.

Fill the tall glasses with ice. Add chocolate bitters (3 dashes per serving) and 1/8 of the infused bourbon. Skewer the Sous vide cherries and garnish.

Serves: 8 **Prep Time: 10mins** **Cook Time: 1 hr**

Calories: 163 **Protein: 0.4g** **Carbs: 2.2g** **Fat: 1.3g**

Watermelon Mint Vodka Infusion

Ingredients

- 1 cup vodka
- 1 cup watermelon, cubed
- 2-3 sprigs fresh mint

Directions

Preheat the water bath to 140°F. Seal all ingredients in a bag. Place in water bath and cook 2 hours. Strain solids from the infusion. Use in your favorite martini recipe.

Serves: 4   **Prep Time: 20mins**   **Cook Time: 2 hrs**

Calories: 140   **Protein: 0.1g**   **Carbs: 17.2g**   **Fat: 0.2g**

Bloody Mary Cocktail

Ingredients:

6 tomatoes, quartered

¼ cup horseradish (from a jar)

¼ cup Worcestershire sauce

2 cups vodka

1 jalapeno pepper, halved, seeded

½ cup lime juice

To serve with:

- Salt, Celery Stalks

Directions

Heat Sous Vide cooker to 145F. In a Sous Vide bag, combine all ingredients.

Seal the bag using water immersion technique. Submerge in water and cook 3 hours.

Remove the bag from the water bath. Strain through a fine-mesh sieve and press the tomatoes to release any remaining pulp. Allow cooling completely before serving. Make a salt rim around the glass. Serve the Bloody Mary in a glass along with a celery stalk.

Serves: 8   **Prep Time: 10mins**   **Cook Time: 3 hrs**

Calories: 150   **Protein: 0.9g**   **Carbs: 6.3g**   **Fat: 0.2g**

Orange-Anise Bitters

Ingredients

- The peel of one orange, pith removed
- 1 star anise
- 1 cup bourbon

Directions

Preheat the water bath to 125°F. Seal all ingredients in a bag and place in water bath. Cook 2 hours. Strain bitters into a small bottle using a coffee filter or a cheesecloth. Before using a cocktail strainer, bring to room temperature.

Serves: 4 **Prep Time: 10mins** **Cook Time: 2 hrs**

Calories: 140 Protein: 0.3g Carbs: 0.06g Fat: 0.2g

Peach Infused Bourbon

Ingredients

- 2 ripe peaches, cut into wedges, pit and peel removed
- 1 cinnamon stick
- 2 cups bourbon

Directions

Preheat the water bath to 150°F. Seal all ingredients in a bag. Place in water bath and cook 2 hours. Strain solids from brandy using a cheesecloth or coffee filter. Bring to room temperature before using in cocktails

Serves: 8   **Prep Time: 20mins**   **Cook Time: 2 hrs**

Calories: 143   **Protein: 0.3g**   **Carbs: 3.58g**   **Fat: 0.1g**

Conclusion

Thank you so much for sticking with us to the end of Sous Vide for Beginners! I hope you have enjoyed all the information we had to share and cooking all 70 recipes with us.

The next step is to continue mixing and matching as you enjoy great food and healthier life. Be sure to join us again on another one of our other amazing culinary adventures, and if you enjoyed my work, go ahead and leave a positive review on my Amazon page!

Until then, keep cooking, and moving towards all your culinary goals. All the best!

DEAR READER,
THANK YOU FOR BUYING AND READING MY BOOK!
IF YOU LIKE IT, PLEASE, LEAVE A REVIEW. IT IS
IMPORTANT FOR ME AND MY FUTURE BOOKS.
JUST SCAN THIS QR CODE AND YOU CAN LEAVE A
REVIEW

OR JUST TYPE THIS LINK –
HTTPS://WWW.AMAZON.COM/REVIEW/CREATE-
REVIEW?IE=UTF8&ASIN=B07B6VB85N#

Copyright 2018 by Melissa Bennett - All rights reserved.

All rights Reserved. No part of this publication or the information in it may be quoted from or reproduced in any form by means such as printing, scanning, photocopying or otherwise without prior written permission of the copyright holder.

Disclaimer and Terms of Use: Effort has been made to ensure that the information in this book is accurate and complete, however, the author and the publisher do not warrant the accuracy of the information, text and graphics contained within the book due to the rapidly changing nature of science, research, known and unknown facts and internet. The Author and the publisher do not hold any responsibility for errors, omissions or contrary interpretation of the subject matter herein. This book is presented solely for motivational and informational purposes only.

Made in the USA
Lexington, KY
20 March 2018